Months of the Year

April

by Mari Kesselring
Illustrated by Brian Caleb Dumm

Content Consultant:
Susan Kesselring, MA
Literacy Educator and Preschool Director

visit us at www.abdopublishing.com

Published by Magic Wagon, a division of the ABDO Group, 8000 West 78th Street, Edina, Minnesota 55439. Copyright © 2010 by Abdo Consulting Group, Inc. International copyrights reserved in all countries

Looking Glass Library™ is a trademark and logo of Magic Wagon.

Printed in the United States.

 PRINTED ON RECYCLED PAPER

Text by Mari Kesselring
Illustrations by Brian Caleb Dumm
Edited by Patricia Stockland
Interior layout and design by Emily Love
Cover design by Emily Love

Library of Congress Cataloging-in-Publication Data
Kesselring, Mari.
  April / by Mari Kesselring ; illustrated by Brian Caleb Dumm ; content consultant, Susan Kesselring.
      p. cm. -- (Months of the year)
   ISBN 978-1-60270-631-6
 1. April (Month)--Juvenile literature. 2. Calendar--Juvenile literature. I. Dumm, Brian Caleb, ill. II. Kesselring, Susan. III. Title.
   CE13.K47 2010
   398'.33--dc22
                                                2008050706

Here is your chance
to learn even more.
What is the name
of month number four?

January

Did you pick a month?

What was your guess?

If you said April,

the answer is yes!

January

February

March

April

May

June

April

July

August

September

October

November

December

5

April comes between
March and May.
This spring month
has 30 fun days!

6

The word *April* used
to mean "open" long ago.
The month has this name because
it's when flowers open and grow.

In April, spring rain
comes pouring down.
Splash in the puddles
you see on the ground!

April Fools' Day is the first,
and people get tricky.
Make sure you don't
sit in something sticky!

13

April is the start
of baseball season.
Go see a game!
You don't need a reason.

Clean a park on Earth Day
to show that you care.
Plant trees on Arbor Day.
They help clean the air!

Passover and Easter are
holidays to celebrate.
Share a meal with your family.
Time together is great!

Grab a pen and some paper.

Do you know why?

April is National Poetry Month.

Give it a try!

It seems April
has come to an end.
But May is waiting
just around the bend!

Write Poems!

April is National Poetry Month. You can practice writing your own poetry. First write down a simple word such as "cat." Then try to think of all the words that end the same as cat. How about hat? Or mat? Can you think of any others?

April Flowers

Plant your own April flowers in your house. Have an adult help you. First, get seeds from the store. Then, get a plastic cup and fill it with dirt. Next, plant a tiny seed in the dirt. Keep it in a sunny spot. Water your flower every day and watch it grow!

Words to Know

bend—a curve in the road.
celebrate—to enjoy something, such as a holiday.
holiday—a special event or celebration that happens every year, such as Easter or Passover.
March—the third month of the year. It comes after February.
May—the fifth month of the year. It comes after April.

Web Sites

To learn more about April, visit ABDO Group online at **www.abdopublishing.com**. Web sites about April are featured on our Book Links page. These links are routinely monitored and updated to provide the most current information available.